Puss and the Birds

Story by Beverley Randell
Illustrated by Betty Greenhatch

Pussy is hungry.
Pussy is looking
for a bird.

Here comes a bird.

Here comes Pussy.

The bird is up in the tree.
The bird is safe.

The birds look down
at Pussy.
"**Naughty Pussy!**
Naughty Pussy!
Naughty Pussy!"

Pussy is hungry.
"Miaow, miaow."

"Come in, Pussy."

"Here you are, Pussy."

Pussy is **not** hungry.

Pussy is up on the bed.

Pussy is asleep.

Cheep, cheep, cheep.
Pussy is asleep.

Pussy is asleep.
Cheep, cheep, cheep.